God is unhappy with the world.
People everywhere lie, and argue, and fight.
"Perhaps I should wash the earth clean," thinks God.

But one good man remains. His name is Noah.
"I'm going to flood the world," God tells him.
"So I want you to build a great boat to keep you safe."

"I will tell you just how to build this boat," says God.
Noah's three sons all help.
They saw, and hammer, and paint.

At last the great ark is finished!
Noah gathers two of every sort of animal.
Two lions, two snakes, two giraffes, and two turtles.

Two butterflies, two pigs, two zebras, and two rabbits.
Noah's three sons help lead the animals into the ark.
At last they're all inside!

Noah, his wife, his sons, and their wives collect food to feed everyone when the flood comes. Black clouds appear.

Everyone goes inside the ark. God shuts the door.
Soon the rain starts. It rains, and rains, and rains!
Now the ark floats on the water.

But Noah, his family, and all the animals are safe inside the ark.
Two parrots, two elephants, two sheep, and two bees.
Two penguins, two chickens, and two goats.

There's plenty for them all to eat and drink.
Noah and his family give food to everyone in the ark.
They are all safe from the great flood.

After forty days and forty nights, the rain stops.
Slowly, slowly, the flood goes down.
Noah sends out a dove. She flies back carrying a green leaf.

Bump! The ark lands on top of a mountain.
Noah opens the door. Out rush all the birds and animals.
God puts a beautiful rainbow in the sky.

"Never again will I flood the whole earth," God promises.
Noah, his family, and all the animals
are saved from the great flood.